Original title:
The Meaning of Life According to Spaghetti

Copyright © 2025 Creative Arts Management OÜ
All rights reserved.

Author: Riley Hawthorne
ISBN HARDBACK: 978-1-80566-095-8
ISBN PAPERBACK: 978-1-80566-390-4

Saucy Revelations

Noodles dance in a pot, so bright,
Giggling and twirling, quite the sight.
Tomato dreams swirl in rich delight,
A splash of joy in every bite.

Parmesan clouds float on high,
Sprinkling wonders as they sigh.
With every slurp, our spirits fly,
Life's a feast, oh me, oh my!

Forks in a Journey

A fork in hand, we set our course,
Twisting through sauce, a flavorful force.
Garlic whispers, the taste, of course,
In this adventure, we find our source.

Al dente roads that gently bend,
Each bite a story, around the bend.
With laughter and noodles, we transcend,
In this pasta life, we'll never end.

Threads of Flavor

Spaghetti strings in a tangle, oh dear,
Like life's odd paths, they wander near.
A sauce of humor, a dash of cheer,
With every slurp, we conquer fear.

Basil dreams and herbs that sway,
In this kitchen, we laugh and play.
The flavor threads guide our way,
Noodling through night and day.

Simmering Reflections

Bubbling thoughts in a pot of gold,
A simmering tale that's fun to behold.
Spaghetti wisdom, daring and bold,
Life's tangled pasta, a story retold.

The ladle stirs, bringing joy to mind,
In this sauce, secret truths we find.
With every bite, our hearts unwind,
In flavors rich, our lives aligned.

Noodle-Lined Paths

On a plate of dreams, we twirl and spin,
Saucy adventures, let the feasting begin.
A strand of joy in every bite,
Laughing as we taste, hearts feel light.

With every slurp, a giggle arises,
Twirled with flavors, no need for disguises.
Life's a banquet served up with cheer,
Pasta's the reason we gather near.

The Sauce of Sentience

Tomato red and basil green,
Pour on the wisdom, life's cuisine.
We dip our bread, thoughts like butter,
In this delicious world, we just stutter.

A sprinkle of cheese, a dash of fun,
We ponder life under the sun.
With every bite, a question to bite,
Why worry at all? Just savor the sight.

Life's Coiling Threads

In pots of bubbling, dreams entwine,
Spaghetti stretches, a twist divine.
Each loop a story, each strand a fate,
We dance on plates, it's never too late.

Forks in hands, laughter flows,
Twisting and turning, where nobody knows.
Life's a dinner, don't take it too hard,
Even the mess is a culinary card.

Endlessly Twisted

We whirl through life like fettuccine,
Sauced with laughter, oh so dreamy.
Every forkful a giggle, yum, what a ride,
Winding our way, with joy as our guide.

In a world so complex, don't take it to heart,
Pasta's perfection, an edible art.
So twirl that noodle, and let spirits soar,
In this buffet of life, there's always room for more.

Flavors of Being

In a pot of water, life does swirl,
Twists and turns, oh what a twirl!
Al dente dreams, just the right bite,
Saucy adventures bring pure delight.

Garlic whispers, spice in the air,
Each bite a giggle, we all share.
Noodles of joy, tangled and free,
A tasty dance, just you and me.

Tasting Transience

Life's a plate, served up quick,
With a dash of humor, take your pick.
Forks of fate, twirl and dive,
In this pasta pot, we thrive!

Tomato sunsets, red so bright,
Slurping laughs, what a sight!
Bite the moment, oh so brief,
Life's a noodle, beyond belief.

The Grains of Gratitude

In every grain, a story lies,
Whispering secrets, oh so wise.
A sprinkle of joy, a pinch of cheer,
Savoring moments, hold them near.

A pasta feast, laughter spills,
Cheesy smiles, and happy thrills.
With every twirl, we celebrate,
Grateful for life on a dinner plate.

Meatballs in Midair

Toss those meatballs, let them fly,
A juggling act in the kitchen sky!
With laughter loud, they bounce and roll,
Spaghetti dreams, they take their toll.

Saucy treasures, flying high,
Watch them dance, oh my, oh my!
A plate of chaos, a comedy,
Life's meatballs bring pure jubilee.

Savoring Simplicity

Twirl the noodles, take a bite,
Sauce drips down, oh what a sight!
Life's a bowl, both rich and plain,
Spaghetti joys will ease the strain.

Forks in hand, we laugh and share,
Each slurp echoes, love is there.
Don't overthink, just take your time,
In every bite, life's little rhyme.

Life Served with Garlic

Garlic whispers to the pasta,
Warmth and laughter come to master.
With a sprinkle of Parmesan gold,
Life's tale is savory and bold.

Pasta parties, friends unite,
Twilight feasts, oh what delight!
Each bite tells a tale to share,
With every noodle, love's in air.

Threads of Tradition

Grandma's recipe held so dear,
Passed down through laughter and cheer.
Twists of fate in a marinara,
Traditions dance like a fireworks flare.

Knead the dough with hands so skilled,
Life's a banquet, not just grilled.
With every plate, memories blend,
A tapestry of joy to send.

A Feast of Experiences

Each noodle tells a tale of dreams,
Saucy escapades, or so it seems.
Spaghetti nights with heartfelt chats,
Life's a feast, and we're the stats!

Tangled moments, laughter bright,
With every bite, we savor light.
Grab a seat, come join the fun,
In this bowl, we all are one.

Melodies of the Spaghetti Bowl

In a pot of water, bubbles dance,
Noodles twirl in a joyful trance,
Sauce drips like laughter, deep and red,
Filling our hearts and our hungry heads.

With a fork in hand, we dive with glee,
Twisting strands as silly as can be,
Tomatoes giggle, garlic claps,
As we slurp up the happy mishaps.

A sprinkle of cheese, a dash of cheer,
Each bite reminds us, bring friends near,
Silly its shape, but I wouldn't trade,
These doughy delights in life's grand parade.

So gather around, let's share the fun,
With a plate of pasta, life's never done,
In every swirl, a laugh we find,
Spaghetti whispers, "Life's kind!"

Spooling Time

Noodles twist in a bowl, oh so grand,
Each twirl a journey, each strand a plan.
Sauce drips like wisdom, savory and bright,
In every bite, there's laughter and light.

Forks dance in quite a silly ballet,
Pasta's a friend that comes out to play.
With each slurp we scream, 'Is this all there is?'
But the answer is buried in garlic and fizz!

Bolognese and Being

Ground beef and tomatoes, a cosmic embrace,
Each simmering bubble, a laugh on our face.
Life's just like pasta, it bends and it breaks,
But with each saucy moment, our humor awakes.

Spilled sauce on my shirt, what a glorious mess,
Each crumb, a reminder that life can impress.
With every rich flavor, we ponder our fate,
Is it all just good food, or something first-rate?

Simmering Questions

As I boil the water, I ponder and muse,
Is there purpose in pasta? What do I choose?
Do meatballs hold answers or just extra zest?
In sauce we find solace, like life's little jest.

With every warm bowl, I'm cheekily fed,
Twirling my thoughts like spaghetti so red.
These questions of being, they bubble and simmer,
In kitchens of laughter, my soul feels much thinner.

The Flavor of Existence

A sprinkle of cheese, a dash of delight,
Every meal a reminder that life can be bright.
From boiling to baking, we savor the ride,
With pasta beside us, there's nothing to hide.

So here's to the noodles, the fun, and the zest,
In every hot dish, we're truly most blessed.
Whether twirled or unraveled, our plates always shine,
In the banquet of life, we know we'll be fine!

Noodles of Existence

In a bowl of twists, we find our way,
As strands connect, we laugh and sway.
Life's like a noodle, long and thin,
Twirling and slurping, let the fun begin!

With every bite, we taste the thrill,
A dash of chaos, a pinch of will.
Saucy moments dance on our lips,
In this pasta journey, we take our trips.

Sauce-Stained Epiphanies

Spilled marinara, a messy delight,
Reminds us life's not just black or white.
In splatters of red, wisdom we find,
Sauce-stained moments, fun intertwined.

As garlic wafts through the air so sweet,
We savor the chaos, we embrace the heat.
A splash of humor, a sprinkle of zest,
With each tasty bite, we're truly blessed.

Twirls of Fate

Twisting and turning, we spin around,
In this pasta dance, we are unbound.
Fate's like a fork, it swirls us near,
In noodles of joy, we shed a tear.

A pinch of luck, a dollop of fun,
With every twirl, there's more to be done.
We twine together, like spaghetti's thread,
In this comedic chaos, we're safely fed.

Al Dente Dreams

Life's a pot, we boil and strain,
With dreams al dente, we'll never abstain.
To chew on the moments, just right, not soft,
We leap for the stars, together we scoff.

Biting through laughter, with flavor in tow,
Our dreams swell high, like pasta in flow.
So let's bake those thoughts, with love in the air,
In this silly banquet, we're beyond compare.

A Dance of Dolce Vita

In water's warm embrace, they twirl,
Noodles spin 'round, a saucy swirl.
Forks take flight, in a joyous chase,
Life's a fête, in each pasta's grace.

Tomato dreams and basil's tease,
With every bite, our hearts find ease.
A sprinkle of cheese, oh what delight,
Dancing through flavors, day and night.

The Unbroken Noodle

In the pot, they stretch and sway,
One long noodle leads the way.
Untangled joy, a twist so bold,
In every loop, a tale unfolds.

No cuts or breaks, just endless fun,
A pasta race that can't be done.
Together they laugh, together they play,
In this pasta world, come what may.

Finding Comfort in Pasta

When days are long and spirits low,
A plate of warmth, the heart will glow.
With every slurp, the frowns all flee,
In bowls of comfort, we find our glee.

Garlic whispers, olive oil's kiss,
Each bite a hug, a moment of bliss.
Pasta's love can never depart,
Fueling joy right from the heart.

Moments Enveloped in Flavor

In a world of spices, we wander free,
Each bite a map, the taste of glee.
Pesto dreams and alfredo nights,
Flavorful hugs in every bite.

A festival of sauce, a cheesy cheer,
With every forkful, all doubt disappears.
Laughing and twirling, our auras bright,
Moments wrapped in flavors ignite.

In the Boiling Pot of Life

In the pot where we all stew,
Life bubbles up, just like we do.
Twists and turns like pasta's dance,
Each flavor mixed, a funny chance.

With a splash of sauce, things get wild,
Forks are flying, laughter's piled.
Taste the moments as they swirl,
Life's a banquet, give it a twirl.

Some days al dente, others mush,
In the chaos, we learn to rush.
But with each strand pulled just right,
We find the joy in every bite.

Gather 'round and raise a cheer,
For every meal makes the heart near.
In the boiling pot, we get the say,
Life's delicious, come join the play.

Stirring Up Memories

As I stir the sauce with a wink,
Memories bubble, let's stop and think.
Each taste recalls a joyful scene,
Mom's recipe, family's cuisine.

Long noodles twist like tales once told,
Every ingredient a memory's hold.
With a pinch of laughter, a dash of cheer,
We savor moments we hold dear.

Garlic sizzles in the pan, oh my!
Add a sprinkle of love, watch it fly!
Life's a dish that's never bland,
Stir it up with a steady hand.

From the pot to the plate, it's a race,
Each serving brings a smile to our face.
Gathered together in a pot so sweet,
Stirring memories makes life complete.

Essence in Every Bite

Twirl your fork, embrace the cheer,
Each noodle holds a story near.
In the sauce lies the truth, you see,
A dash of joy, a splash of glee.

With every bite, we journey far,
To feasts and laughs beneath the stars.
Spices tickle the taste buds just right,
Life's a buffet, such a delight!

Fettuccine dreams and ravioli schemes,
Each flavor whispering secret themes.
A sprinkle of cheese, a twist of fate,
Every mouthful is worth the wait.

So slurp it up, don't let it slide,
In this realm, we take our stride.
Essence captured in every bite,
With silly joy, we shine so bright.

Pastabilities Unfold

In the world of pasta, dreams are shaped,
With every twist, new paths are draped.
From spaghetti strands to gnocchi bliss,
Funny tales in every twist and hiss.

With marinara dreams and pesto schemes,
Life is saucy, bursting at the seams.
Slicing garlic, we laugh and sing,
Creating magic is a tasty thing.

Each sauce tells a story so bold,
Of laughter, love, adventures untold.
From the pot to our fork, we find it true,
Pastabilities are endless, just like our crew.

So embrace the noodles, let the fun flow,
With silly moments that steal the show.
In this banquet of joy, we find a way,
To celebrate life, come join the play!

Strands of Purpose

In a pot of boiling cheer,
We find purpose, oh so clear.
Twist and twirl, life's a dance,
With every noodle, take a chance.

Sauce drips down, it's a delight,
Filling our bowls, oh what a sight!
Life's made of flavors, rich and pure,
Each strand we slurp, we feel secure.

Forking Paths

With a fork in hand, we face the choice,
Do we spin or do we rejoice?
Life's messy with drips and spills,
Yet every bite brings joyous thrills.

Twisty roads, they make us laugh,
Saucy tales on our pasta path.
Noodles tangle, but who cares?
The joy of flavor, love, and shares.

A Journey Through Tomato Fields

In lands of ripe, red tomato bliss,
We chase the tang of a savory kiss.
Fields stretch wide under sunlit skies,
Harvesting laughter, each bite applies.

Rolling in sauce, with a giggle or two,
Sun-kissed fruit, dreams come true.
Life is best when seasoned right,
A sprinkle of joy to take our flight.

The Pasta Paradox

Two noodles meet in a puzzling twist,
One says, "What's the foodie list?"
The other sighs, "Let's not debate,
Just slurp it up before it's late!"

A paradox of shapes and taste,
In a world of carbs, who can waste?
Embrace the chaos, don't be shy,
Pasta makes everything less dry!

Noodle Knots of Wisdom

In a pot of boiling dreams,
Twirl the strings, it seems,
Life's a dance, a saucy whirl,
Pasta twirls, oh the twirl!

Each noodle bends, it pretends,
Silly shapes that never end,
Sometimes straight, then curly too,
Life's just one big tasty stew.

Don't forget the sprinkle cheer,
Parmesan, to add some flair,
With every bite, a secret told,
Life's better served, with cheese tenfold.

So boil and toss, embrace the fun,
Each squiggly twist, a life well spun,
In every fork, a giggle bright,
Noodle knots bring pure delight.

Sauced Success

In a world where meatballs roll,
Sauces pour, they take their toll,
Tomato dreams and garlic sighs,
Spaghetti lifts us to the skies.

Slurp and slosh, a joyful sound,
As flavor melds, it knows no bound,
The pasta whispers in delight,
For sauce will make everything right.

Stir the pot, embrace the splash,
Life's a dish, so make a dash,
With every bite, a chuckle grows,
Sauced up moments, that's how life flows.

So grab your fork, join in the zest,
Life is better when you're blessed,
With noodles rich and laughter sweet,
Saucy evenings can't be beat!

Strands of Serendipity

Tangled strands, life's embrace,
Pasta twists in a playful race,
Unexpected bites, a laugh we share,
With every slurp, we show we care.

Laughter bubbles in the pot,
Serendipity is what we've got,
Sauce drips down, a vibrant art,
Every noodle plays its part.

In tangled knots, we find our way,
A savory journey, come what may,
With flavors bold and stories grand,
Every meal, a life well planned.

So twirl and taste, don't let it stray,
Embrace the mess, live the way,
For in each strand, joy's not far,
Noodle tales are who we are!

Spirals of Significance

In spirals dance, our lives align,
Noodles twist, a grand design,
Every loop a tale to tell,
In pasta shapes, we find our spell.

Beneath the sauce, a treasure hides,
In every curve, a secret bides,
Life's a dish, not made for stress,
Twist and twirl, embrace the mess.

With garlic dreams and basil zest,
In every bite, we find the best,
Noodle in, and laugh out loud,
In spirals, we're a laughter crowd.

So take your plate, don't hesitate,
Mix it up, it's never too late,
For in each twist, life's joys appear,
Spirals of fun, we hold so dear.

Aromatic Awakening

In the pot, a dance begins,
Noodles swirl like playful twins.
Tomato sauce, a splash of cheer,
Whispers, "Join me, have no fear!"

Garlic dances, fragrant and bright,
Spices tease, a pure delight.
Bubbling laughter fills the air,
Life's a feast if you dare to share!

Forks are flying, noodles twirl,
Sauce drips down, a messy whirl.
Every bite, a joyful sound,
In this chaos, joy is found!

So take a seat, don't be shy,
Life's too short for a plain pie.
With every slurp, we rise and sing,
In the world of pasta, we're all kings!

A Feast for Thought

In a bowl of joy, we dive,
Splashes of color come alive.
Pasta dreams and cheese atop,
A mountain feast, we munch and stop!

Silly shapes of spirals and bows,
Tell the stories life bestows.
Mix it up, add a twist,
In this mess, we coexist!

With every sauce, a tale unfolds,
Of adventures shared and laughter bold.
No need for forks, just dig right in,
Spaghetti victories, where do we begin?

So raise your plate, let's toast tonight,
To all the flavors, wrong and right.
Life's a banquet, come and munch,
In the world of pasta, let's all brunch!

Life's Recipe Unraveled

From flour and water, life commenced,
A twist of fate, a noodle dense.
Knead it softly, let it rest,
In a world of carbs, we are blessed!

Boiling water, bubbling fun,
Watch the chaos, oh what a run!
Once it's soft, toss in some zest,
Each plate a canvas, we are guests!

Ladle on sauce, a splash of flair,
Cheesy goodness, beyond compare.
With meatballs rolling, laughter flies,
In spaghetti dreams, our spirits rise!

A table spread, the friends all cheer,
With every bite, we lose our fear.
So grab your fork and twirl with glee,
In life's grand feast, just let it be!

The Essence of Elbows

Elbow pasta, curvy and sly,
Trying its best to catch the eye.
A playful twist, a saucy friend,
In this dish, the fun won't end!

With cheese that melts and hugs each curve,
Every bite's got the right serve.
Steaming bowls and laughter loud,
In this moment, let's be proud!

So bring your forks, let's dig right in,
In sauce we trust, let love begin.
With each slurp and playful cheer,
Life's a party when carbs are near!

So twirl that spoon, don't hold back,
In noodle land, we're on the right track.
To taste and share, that's the key,
In pasta's world, we're fancy free!

Lesson in Every Forkful

In a pot where noodles sway,
Each twist a lesson, come what may.
Saucy dreams in every bite,
Laughing at woes, oh what a sight!

Spaghetti strands, a tangled mess,
Life's a riddle, we must confess.
With marinara, our fears are masked,
In this bowl of joy, we are basked!

A sprinkle of cheese, a dash of fun,
Together we eat, together we run.
Forks raised high, to the sky we cheer,
Finding truth in each tasty sphere!

So twirl it right, don't let it fall,
In laughter and joy, we'll have it all.
Each slurp and noodle, a comical ride,
Life's a feast, let's enjoy the tide!

Life Tossed with Olive Oil

With olive oil drizzled wide,
We sauté our hopes, let dreams collide.
Garlic whispers, sizzle and pop,
Life's a dance, we never stop!

Toss in laughter, sprinkle some zest,
Each day unfolds, a savory quest.
Basil kisses the playful air,
In this pan, we've not a care!

Serve it up with a side of glee,
Noodles twist, wild and free.
With every bite, we celebrate,
Embracing each flavor on our plate!

A splash of joy, a pinch of cheer,
In the kitchen of life, we persevere.
So gather round, let's share the meal,
In these moments, our souls can heal!

Spirals of Self-Discovery

In spirals of pasta, we learn and grow,
Every twirl shows us where to go.
Pondering life with a fork in hand,
Noodle tales are simply grand!

The more we mix, the more we find,
Silly secrets left behind.
In marinara rivers, we dive so deep,
Waking up truths that we keep!

So boil with dreams, simmer in cheer,
With each strand, we shed a tear.
Tangled knots, yet laughter flows,
In spaghetti, true wisdom shows!

With every bite, a story spun,
Life's a noodle, let's have fun.
Serve it warm with love and grace,
In every forkful, we find our place!

Garnished with Gratitude

A plate adorned with colorful flair,
We gather round, a love to share.
With each noodle, we write our song,
In this pasta life, we all belong!

Basil and garlic, flavors unite,
Grateful hearts in a warm candlelight.
As we feast, let laughter ring,
In spaghetti's embrace, we find our spring!

Topped with joy, and smiles so bright,
Each meal reminds us to hold on tight.
With sauce so rich and stories bold,
In every bite, true love unfolds!

So raise your forks, let's toast our fate,
In this banquet, we celebrate.
With gratitude sprinkled, our spirits soar,
Life's a banquet, let's eat some more!

Whispers of Wheat

In a pot of boiling cheer,
Noodles dance without a fear.
Twirl them round, so full of glee,
Each strand whispers mysteries.

Pasta dreams of marinara,
A saucy life, not just a rara.
With meatballs round, so robust and bold,
The secret's out, or so I'm told.

Al dente or just plain mush?
In a slurp, we find the rush.
Live to twirl, let sauce ignite,
In noodle we trust, it feels just right.

So grab a fork, and do not wait,
For pasta secrets, life is great.
In every bite, there's joy to find,
A bowl of laughter, all entwined.

The Spaghetti Paradox

A noodle's loop, a twist of fate,
Is life a meal or just a plate?
Sauce drips down, a joyous plight,
Each slurp reveals more appetite.

Twisted thoughts in fibers thick,
With every bite, we choose our trick.
A plate of carbs, yet light as air,
What's food for thought becomes a prayer.

With garlic breath and laughter shared,
We question if the chef has dared.
To mix the mundane with the divine,
In every bite, we taste the line.

So sing the praises, toss the greens,
For life's a pasta with endless scenes.
In every fork, find joy anew,
A paradox, so true and gooey too.

Glistening Moments

Behold the strands, so silk and bright,
Drenched in dreams, a lovely sight.
Each twirl's a wish, a hope, a cheer,
In every bite, we shed a tear.

Fragrant herbs set spirits free,
The pot's a cauldron of jubilee.
A sprinkle here, a dash of fun,
We gather 'round, the feast begun.

With laughter bubbling, sauce aglow,
Little moments, how they flow.
Tangled tales on plates we share,
In pasta we find love laid bare.

So lift your fork, and raise a glass,
Celebrate these moments, let them last.
In every meal, pure joy will gleam,
Life's a noodle — chase the dream!

A Bowl of Purpose

In bowls of joy, we scoop and swirl,
Pasta spins, a ribboned whirl.
Every sauce tells tales untold,
A bowl of purpose, bright and bold.

With parmesan rains, we sprinkle cheer,
Gather 'round, for friends are near.
As noodles hug, and laughter soars,
Life's greatest moments in sauce, not chores.

Each bite a laughter, a truth, a jest,
Who knew that noodles could be the best?
With forks in hand, we take a stand,
In every dish, a tale so grand.

So raise a toast to pasta dreams,
Life's a bowl bursting at the seams.
In flavors deep, our purpose shines,
With every meal, our joy aligns.

Life in Exciting Stir-Fry

In the pan with a sizzle and pop,
Noodles twirl and dance non-stop.
Veggies leap in joy, oh what a sight,
A whirl of flavors, pure delight!

Sauce drips like laughter, a sticky treat,
Together we feast, life is sweet.
A dash of spice, a pinch of glee,
In this pot, we're wild and free!

Forks in hand, we slurp and sway,
Every bite brings a brand new play.
With noodles long and stories vast,
Life's a feast that's meant to last!

So let's stir this bowl with all our might,
In the kitchen, everything feels right.
Add a sprinkle of joy, a splash of cheer,
With each tasty bite, we lose our fear!

Entangled in Curves

Twisted shapes that make us grin,
Fettuccine fun, let the games begin!
Bouncing spaghetti, swirling round,
Life's a noodle, joy unbound!

In bowls of laughter, we dive and twirl,
Pasta parties, watch the sauce swirl.
Entangled in curves, we find our way,
With every slurp, we laugh and play!

Pasta al dente, just like our dreams,
Soggy life? Not as it seems.
We twine together, friends so dear,
A noodle bond, bring on the cheer!

So grab your forks, let's make a scene,
With every bite, we'll ketchup (catch up) keen.
In this spaghetti realm, oh what a ride,
Life's a noodle; let's enjoy the glide!

Filling the Bowl of Being

A big bowl waits, full to the brim,
Life's pasta party, let's not be grim.
With every scoop, the joy increases,
Warm and cozy, all fears cease.

Tomato sauce like a warm embrace,
Filling the bowl, we find our place.
Garlic whispers secrets in the air,
Life's a feast; let's share and care!

Twirling noodles, a dance of fate,
Gather 'round, it's never too late.
With each bite we take, memories flow,
Filling this bowl with love, we grow!

So serve it up, let's fill the night,
With noodles and laughter, all feels right.
In every scoop, let's find our song,
A bowl of being where we belong!

Pesto Dreams

In a jar of green, dreams lay in wait,
Basil whispers, "Life's pretty great!"
Walnuts crunching, garlic's delight,
Stirring up laughter, our future's bright!

Pesto dreams swirl in our minds,
As we twirl spaghetti, joy we find.
Cheese rains down, golden and fine,
Each bite bursts with flavors divine!

Life's a canvas, painted with sauce,
Pesto adventures, no need for gloss.
Colorful plates, a savory scheme,
Waking each taste bud, a true dream!

So let's whip up some joy tonight,
With pesto dreams, life feels just right.
In the kitchen of fun, let's never stop,
For every meal brings a reason to hop!

Seasoned Moments

In a pot of boiling dreams, we twirl,
Noodles dance, a pasta swirl,
Sauce splashes with joy so bright,
Every bite feels just right.

Garlic whispers in the air,
Cheese cascades without a care,
Life's moments, like al dente strands,
Slips through fingers, not in hands.

Around the table, laughter spreads,
Forks and fables, no time for beds,
Salad greens on the side, oh please,
Life's troubles vanish with a tease.

So let's indulge in this delight,
Together we'll feast, hearts feel light,
With every twirl, let's celebrate,
As noodles weave our fate so great.

Spaghetti Connections

Twirled around, we share a meal,
Every strand a secret deal,
Garlic bread, a crunchy friend,
In this bowl, the fun won't end.

Laughter flows like marinara,
Jokes get tangled, oh what a gala,
Fettuccine dreams on plates abound,
In every bite, joy can be found.

A meaty tale, a veggie tease,
With a sprinkle of humor, life's a breeze,
In this pasta paradise, we stay,
Tangled up in a friendly way.

So raise your forks to love and cheer,
Surrounded by those we hold dear,
In every noodle, a tale unspooled,
Together we thrive, and life's renewed.

Twists and Turns of Destiny

Life's a noodle, long and twisty,
Sauced with laughter, never misty,
Every bend brings something new,
Like spaghetti, we'll push on through.

Alfredo's dreams, a cheesy fate,
Our stories simmer, never late,
With each curve, a fork in the road,
Pasta paths lighten the load.

A meatball here, a sauce so bold,
Tales of adventures, fun to be told,
Twists will come, good times persist,
In this plate of joys, we coexist.

So grab a plate, take a chance,
Join the noodles in a dance,
With each slurp, our dreams collide,
In this spaghetti life, we take pride.

A Culinary Canvas

Life's a canvas, splashed with sauce,
Noodles, colors, no sense of loss,
Each ingredient tells a tale,
From tomato reds to herb-filled trails.

Pasta shapes, a work of art,
With every dish, we play our part,
A pinch of humor, salt a dash,
Together we create a splash.

On this plate, we all belong,
Stirred with laughter, a hearty song,
Each meal a masterpiece to savor,
With love as the main flavor.

So let's paint with forks and knives,
Creating memories, vibrant lives,
In each bite, our dreams expand,
Spaghetti's magic at our hand.

A Culinary Map

In a pot of water, dreams start to swell,
Twisting and turning, they weave a tale.
Spaghetti's dance, a joy to behold,
Stories of flavors, in noodles so bold.

Al dente adventures, with sauce so fine,
Each bite a giggle, a taste divine.
Garlic whispers secrets, while herbs sing loud,
Under the kitchen light, we feel so proud.

Forks swirl like wands, casting pasta dreams,
With every slurp, we're bursting at the seams.
Cheese rains down like sprinkles of joy,
A plate of laughter, not just for a boy.

So throw in some veggies, let's make it a feast,
A noodleful life, from west to east.
Each twirl of spaghetti, a reason to cheer,
With every bite sampled, we shed every fear.

Noodleful Narratives

Once upon a time, in a boiling pot,
Noodles danced madly, like wonder sought.
Each twist a giggle, each curve a glee,
In the kingdom of pasta, we're wild and free.

Sauce splashed stories, rich with delight,
Tomato tales twinkled in neapolitan light.
A sprinkle of cheese, a dash of fate,
In the noodle realm, life can't be late.

Let's gather around, with forks held high,
Slurping spaghetti as the hours fly by.
With a sauce of humor and wisdom so grand,
In the world of noodles, together we stand.

So twirl up a yarn, let's banish the gloom,
In a bowl full of dreams, we're forever in bloom.
Pasta's our ticket to laughs and to cheer,
With every last noodle, we hold life dear.

Hearts in a Bowl

Beneath the moonlight, a bowl full of cheer,
Noodles unite hearts that gather near.
With each little bite, connection grows tight,
In this comedy kitchen, everything's right.

Spaghetti hugs join like friends in a pact,
Mixing and mingling, there's no need to act.
Garlic and herbs, a flavorful team,
Taking the mundane, and making it scream!

Pour on the sauce, let the giggles flow,
Each twirl and toss ignites the show.
Slippery noodles, they dance on the tongue,
In this quirky life, we're forever young.

So gather your loved ones, no time to waste,
With hearts in a bowl, it's a flavorful haste.
Let laughter be dressing, on pasta we feast,
In the warmth of the kitchen, we're all released.

Savory Secrets

Under the lid, where the magic stirs,
Noodles share secrets, bright as the furs.
Swirling and twirling, a mystery's tease,
In the pot of wonders, we find our ease.

With every log of pasta, a giggle ignites,
Laughing with sauce, through long, cozy nights.
Basil and thyme, on this culinary quest,
In the land of spaghetti, we feel truly blessed.

Laughter's the ingredient, that pulls us along,
In the melody of noodles, we all belong.
So let's lift our forks, and toast to the fun,
In the savory secret, our hearts weigh a ton.

Each plate a canvas, with flavors galore,
In the festival of taste, there's always more.
Join in the laughter, let's wiggle and sway,
With spaghetti around, who needs a buffet?

Strung Together

In a pot of water, dreams arise,
Twisting and curling, much to our surprise.
Beneath the bubbles, laughter spills,
Pasta's dance ignites our thrills.

Noodles long and never shy,
They link us all, oh my, oh my!
With each forkful, stories weave,
Together we laugh and believe.

Sauce drips like life's big mess,
A splash of joy, a dash of stress.
But through it all, we share a plate,
Forever friends, it's never too late.

So twirl your spaghetti, don't be a bore,
In the bowl of existence, there's always more.
Let's sauce it up, with giggles aplenty,
In strands of pasta, we find the gentry.

A Life Less Sauced

They say go easy on the cream,
But who wants a life that's bland, it seems?
Without a splash of flavor near,
Our days would vanish, what a queer idea!

So every bite is an ode to fun,
Fling your noodles, don't just stun!
Add a sprinkle of spice, a dash of zest,
In our unwound lives, we are truly blessed.

A pinch of salt, a squeeze of lime,
With each light-hearted jest, we rhyme.
No need for formalities, just dive in,
In this saucy chaos, let the fun begin!

Let's stir the pot, mix dreams on our plate,
Laughter's the sauce, oh isn't it great?
Forget your worries, take a chance—
In every noodle, life's silly dance.

Tasting Joy in Every Bite

Pasta bows in a cheerful swirl,
A forkful of giggles—life's great pearl.
Bite after bite, joy multiplies,
In cheesy bliss, our spirits rise.

With each twirl, we savor delight,
In garlic whispers, our hearts take flight.
Saucy tales glaze every thread,
Taste the laughter, let it spread.

Life's a buffet, come take your share,
With spaghetti in hand, we're without a care.
A savory hug in each wormy strand,
Together we feast, across this grand land.

So laugh and twirl, don't hesitate,
In every mouthful, happiness awaits.
Dig into the joy, let flavors unite,
As we dine on dreams, shining bright.

Garlicky Graces

Garlic wafts through the kitchen air,
A tender kiss of love laid bare.
In a skillet sizzle, we find delight,
Noodles whisper secrets in the night.

With butter and herbs, we craft our fate,
A pinch of chaos, a sprinkle of fate.
Slurps and giggles fill every room,
In our pasta party, there's always room.

So toss the pasta, let flavors collide,
In this garlicky embrace, we'll never hide.
With each savory slurp, our worries depart,
In the noodle whirl, we warm our heart.

So let's raise our forks to this crazy life,
A skewer of laughter amid all the strife.
With squeezes of lemon and drizzles of cheer,
Spaghetti binds us, year after year.

Saucy Journey

In a pot of simmering dreams,
Noodles twist in vibrant beams.
Sauce flows like tales untold,
Each strand a whimsy, brave and bold.

A sprinkle of cheese, a dash of flair,
Life's banquet served without a care.
Twirl your fork, embrace the fun,
In this savory race, we always run.

Garlic whispers secrets sweet,
On this plate, our hearts will meet.
With every bite, a chuckle shared,
Spaghetti teaches us—who's prepared?

So let the pasta dance and sing,
Together, let's enjoy this fling.
For in each slurp and joyful chime,
We find our rhythm, soft as thyme.

The Enigma of Ingredients

Tomatoes squish with vibrant glee,
Winking at us, come, look and see.
Olive oil glistens, a golden sheen,
What magic lies in this cuisine?

Basil's perfume wraps the air,
A mystery of flavors, everywhere.
A pinch of salt from far-off shores,
In this pot, life's essence pours.

Bouncing noodles, crazy and wild,
Childlike laughter, joy-denied child.
Is it fate or just a twist?
At the table, we can't resist.

With each layer, a story spins,
As we savor, the giggles begin.
Tangled together, we laugh and muse,
In this bowl, we simply choose.

Communal Plates

Gather 'round, it's time to feast,
In laughter's light, our worries ceased.
Forks collide, and sauce takes flight,
A dance of flavors, pure delight.

Pass the cheese, let's make it rain,
Our mouths can't help but smile in vain.
Sharing strands, we grasp with glee,
In this moment, we all agree.

Spaghetti strings symbolize us,
Tangled together, without a fuss.
From family ties to friends anew,
Each bite a hug, life's love comes through.

With laughter loud and joy in spades,
We feast like champs on our homemade braids.
So let's communalize our plates,
With pasta love, the heart celebrates!

Bites of Reflection

As noodles swirl in a fragrant haze,
We ponder life in silly ways.
With every slurp, a truth unveiled,
This whimsical feast cannot be derailed.

Meatballs roll like merry thoughts,
In savory pools where laughter's caught.
Sometimes tangled, sometimes free,
Each forkful brings epiphany.

A spoonful of sauce, a dash of cheer,
In this bowl, we conquer fear.
And with each bite, our worries flee,
In pasta there's serenity.

So raise your glasses, toast aloud,
To all the moments, life's so proud.
In our hearts, forever thrive,
Lessons learned with every dive.

A Pasta Portrait

In a bowl of noodles, we find our fate,
Twisted and saucy, it's never too late.
Strands of our dreams, all piled so high,
Slurping down goodness, we laugh and we sigh.

Meatballs roll by like little round suns,
Dancing on parmesan, oh what fun!
Each twirl of the fork takes us for a spin,
No forks in the road, just let the feast begin!

Garlic bread whispers, 'Come join my crew,'
Where life gets saucy, and laughs are too.
With each glimmering bite, joy fills the plate,
In pasta we trust, it's never too late.

So raise up your spaghetti, let's toast to our fate,
In sauce we find friendship, oh, isn't it great?
With laughter and noodles, what more can we crave?
In this tasty portrait, we find what we save.

Tangles of Time

Life's like a noodle — it bends and it sways,
It tangles and twirls in whimsical ways.
With each twist and turn, there's pasta delight,
In every rendition, all feels just right.

In timers that tick, we boil and we strain,
Checking the pot while we dance in the rain.
When a noodle's overcooked, don't fret, don't despair,
Just add in some sauce, and we'll fix up our flair.

Forks at the ready, the clock's running fast,
What's served on our plate, oh, how it's amassed!
Each bite tells a story, each slurp is a rhyme,
Together we laugh through these tangles of time.

So twirl with abandon, let flavors collide,
In this pasta buffet, there's no need to hide.
As we savor each moment, our hearts take flight,
With every noodle shared, life feels just right.

Served with Intention

A sprinkle of laughter sits atop every plate,
Each slice of garlic bread seals our fate.
In sauces of colors, we find our cheer,
With laughter as seasoning, we'll always be near.

Life's a feast served hot, with a wink and a grin,
Where noodles unite us, let's dig right in!
With pesto or marinara, choose your delight,
In this hearty embrace, everything feels right.

Let's twirl up our dreams on a fork made of hope,
Together we savor, together we cope.
Some spill their stories, but oh what a splash,
In servings of joy, we find our heart's cache.

So here's to each noodle, so simple, so grand,
In this pasta connection, we all understand.
With intentions so pure, and laughter aligned,
We're served up with flavor, so joyfully entwined.

Bolognese Beacons

In a pot bubbling bright, hope simmers and brews,
With garlic and onions, we dance to the tunes.
A splash of red wine, adds a touch of flair,
With bolognese beacons, we lighten the air.

Each ladle of sauce is a story we tell,
As dreams float and swirl like a flavorful spell.
In noodles we journey, through laughter and tears,
In savory moments that banish our fears.

Twirling our pasta, we lighten the load,
Finding joy in each bite, as we share the road.
A recipe crafted with love and delight,
In bolognese beacons, we shine ever bright.

So gather 'round tables, bring forks, it's our time,
With pasta in hand, we feel truly sublime.
In the warmth of good cheer, we've nothing to lack,
With bolognese whispers, we'll never look back.

Saucy Revelations

In a pot of water, dreams take a dive,
Swirling like thoughts, they dance and jive.
Tomato, garlic, a simmering play,
Life's saucy secrets bubble away.

Meatballs ponder, 'What's our role?'
Do we stir hearts, or just fill a bowl?
A pinch of humor, a dash of zest,
In this noodle world, we're all just guests.

Twisting and turning, the pasta knows,
Each curve and twist, where laughter flows.
With every forkful, giggles unfurl,
Life's a banquet; come join the whirl!

So slurp up joy, let your worries slide,
With every bite, let good times ride.
In sauce and noodles, truth takes its shape,
Life is a feast, no room for drape.

Delicate Threads of Being

A strand of noodle, so thin, so bright,
Each twist a story, a spark of light.
In boiling water, we find our groove,
Life's delicate dance, made to move.

With butter and cheese, a silky embrace,
Every bite savored, in this crazy race.
Together we simmer, apart we dry,
Like pasta and sauce, we flourish and fly.

Through forks and spaghetti, we find our place,
A noodle community, oh what a space!
With laughter and love, we spiral so free,
In bowls of joy, there's always a spree.

So here's to the sauce, the glories we chase,
In life's grand kitchen, we all share a base.
With every twirl, let's wiggle and sing,
For in each bowl, life's joys take wing.

The Alchemy of Ingredients

Take flour and water, a miracle starts,
Kneaded with laughter, it warms our hearts.
From humble beginnings, we rise and we bend,
In the alchemy of life, there's always a blend.

Olive oil whispers, 'Let's sauté our dreams,'
Garlic and onions, bursting at the seams.
A dash of humor, a sprinkle of cheer,
In this cooking pot, there's nothing to fear.

As spices mingle, they giggle and dance,
Creating a flavor that puts you in a trance.
With spoons and forks, we taste and we share,
In this culinary chaos, we find that we care.

So toss in the laughter, let joy simmer slow,
In every red sauce, a vibrant glow.
Life's a recipe, let's make it divine,
For in every bite, we find the sublime.

Bowls of Contemplation

In a bowl of pasta, thoughts swirl around,
Sinking like meatballs, to be joyfully found.
Each slurp a question, a curious quest,
What makes us human? The sauce or the zest?

Pasta dreams serve, like fortune cookies,
Twisting and twirling, so many rookies!
With every noodle, a new thought is spun,
Does life taste better shared under the sun?

From spaghetti to fettuccine, a dance of fate,
We mingle and blend, oh isn't it great?
With laughter as seasoning, spice things just right,
In the kitchen of life, let's savor each bite.

So grab a fork, let's dive in tonight,
With bowls of contemplation, we'll laugh in delight.
Life's quirks and pasta, they swirl and they play,
In a feast of reflection, we find our way.

A Recipe for Understanding

In the pot, we swirl and twirl,
Noodles dancing, a bouncy whirl.
Sauce drips down with a giggle and grin,
Life tastes better when shared with kin.

Al dente dreams, just the right bite,
Add a pinch of humor, make it light.
Simmered slowly, let flavors meld,
In seasons of joy, our hearts are held.

Measuring out each twist and turn,
With every spoonful, new lessons we learn.
Garlic and basil begin the race,
Life's best moments, we gladly embrace.

So grab a fork, let's take a dive,
In this pasta dish, we truly thrive.
With laughter served on a warm plate,
Understanding grows, oh so great!

Tomato Triumph

A plump red fruit with a zestful cheer,
Spicy tales in every sphere.
Sizzle and pop in the bubbling vat,
Tomatoes beat sadness, how about that?

With every chop, a story unfolds,
Saucy secrets, worth more than gold.
They giggle and wiggle in the pan,
Reminding us life's part of the plan.

Throw in some spices for a dash of glee,
Each bite is a riddle, just wait and see.
In each tomato, a moment so bright,
Cooking is joy, a simple delight.

So toast to the fruit in our tasty show,
With tomato triumph, our spirits will glow.
In every jar, love is preserved,
In this saucy life, we're finally served!

A Whirlwind of Flavor

Twirl those noodles in endless flight,
Sauce sings a song in the warm, soft light.
Dancing on plates, a culinary dance,
Life's a buffet, let's take a chance.

Garlic whirls with a twist of fate,
Spaghetti strands, they never wait.
With every slurp and a contented sigh,
We find our bliss, oh my, oh my!

A sprinkle of cheese, a dash of flair,
Life's unexpected, but we're unaware.
In the chaos, familiarity reigns,
Like pasta twists in intimate chains.

So pass me the fork, let's dig right in,
With each bite, let the laughter begin.
In this whirlwind, we find our place,
Life's just pasta, wrapped in warm grace.

Doused in Possibility

A platter of dreams, a feast so wide,
Topped with the hopes we all cannot hide.
Every sauce tells a story true,
Doused in possibility, just for you.

From pesto green to marinara red,
Life's flavors dance, never misled.
Stirring together what we hold near,
In the pot of existence, let's persevere.

Twists and turns, oh the shapes we make,
Life's full of surprises, with every break.
With laughter and sauce, we'll conquer the day,
In this oodles of noodles, hip-hip-hooray!

So grab your spoon and take a taste,
In the bowl of life, let's never waste.
Each twirl's a blessing, each bite divine,
In this pasta party, you're truly mine!

Culinary Conundrums

In a pot of boiling glee,
Noodles dance, oh so free.
Twirl them high, let them fly,
What's the secret? Don't ask why.

Tomato sauce spills with zest,
Even chefs can't stand the stress.
Garlic whispers, 'Do not fret!'
Life's a feast, don't you forget.

Forks vs. spoons, the great debate,
Round and round, it's dinner fate.
A twist, a twirl, it's all delight,
Pasta dreams in every bite.

If life gets saucy, let it drip,
Savor flavors, take a trip.
In each bite, a giggle's found,
Spaghetti's joy will turn you round.

Of Heart and Pasta.

A heart-shaped ravioli glows,
Love is served—everybody knows.
Each bite a hug, warm and tight,
Carb-loaded dreams throughout the night.

With basil leaves, we toast the day,
A sprinkle here, a dash, hooray!
When life gets tough, we twirl and dive,
With marinara, we feel alive.

Al dente thoughts in saucy streams,
Life is more than what it seems.
In every slurp, a smile's made,
In pasta we find our escapade.

So gather 'round the table wide,
Together with noodles, we'll abide.
With laughter and a butter swirl,
Life's a party; give it a whirl!

Noodles of Existence

Twisted shapes and silly strands,
Life's a pot, with many hands.
From fettuccine to spaghet,
Embrace the silliness, don't forget.

Bubbling waters, giddy flows,
What's the score? No one knows.
Pasta lives in every heart,
A noodle tale, a work of art.

Forks are mighty, spoons are sly,
Making memories as we try.
In every bite, we dance and spin,
Noodle visions make us grin.

Saucy laughter fills the air,
Pasta joys we all can share.
When life gets tough, just take a stand,
And twirl those noodles, it's all planned.

Sauce-Splattered Wisdom

A splash of sauce, a wobbly dish,
Life is served, fulfill a wish.
With garlic bread on the side,
In a world of carbs, we all abide.

Fumbling forks and clumsy spills,
Noodle dreams and cheesy thrills.
Sprinkle magic, pesto cheer,
In the chaos, joy draws near.

Lasagna layers, deep and wide,
Between the sheets, our dreams collide.
Every bite tells a grand affair,
Sauce-splattered wisdom hangs in air.

So laugh and twirl, don't mind the mess,
In pasta life, we'll all confess.
A twinkling wink, a pasta twist,
In this feast, joy can't be missed.

Culinary Chronicles

In a pot of bubbles, it spins and swirls,
Mingling with sauces, putting on twirls.
Every twist tells a story, every noodle a tale,
With a sprinkle of cheese, we set our sail.

With garlic and herbs, the flavors will dance,
In the kitchen's warm glow, we find our chance.
Slurping and laughing, we savor the chase,
In this noodle experiment, we find our place.

A forkful of joy, a plate piled high,
Chasing the pasta, oh my, oh my!
Each bite a delight, a cheerful embrace,
In this bowl of goodness, we find our grace.

So let's boil our dreams, let the sauce run free,
With spaghetti as guide, we laugh and we see.
In life served al dente, the fun's just begun,
With noodles as mentors, we laugh, we run.

Spaghetti Holders of Hope

Twirl the spaghetti, let it take flight,
In a world of sauce, everything feels right.
With meatballs of courage, we'll conquer our fear,
Each mouthful a hug, bringing laughter near.

Noodles like ribbons, draping with flair,
A feast of endurance, cooked with care.
Chews of determination, slurps of delight,
In the kitchen's embrace, everything's bright.

With a pinch of salt, we sprinkle some cheer,
As we twirl on this journey, let's bring friends near.
From pot to our plates, connections ignite,
In this bowl of wisdom, we all feel light.

So grab a long strand, hold on to the fun,
In this pasta-filled world, we've already won.
With each joyful slurp, we savor this dance,
In life's noodle quest, we find our chance.

The Pot of Possibilities

In the bubbling pot, dreams boil away,
Spaghetti spaghetti, come join the fray.
With flavors of garlic and hints of delight,
Each twirl is a promise our futures are bright.

A gathering platter, where laughter does flow,
With olive oil drizzles, we watch spirits glow.
Let's slip on our forks, dive deep and explore,
In the treasure of pasta, there's always much more.

Beneath every sauce, there's a secret inspired,
A pinch of adventure, in noodles we're wired.
Twirling in tandem, let flavors collide,
In this culinary ride, let joy be our guide.

So dance with your fork, take a bite full of fun,
In this pot of dreams, we've already begun.
A life lesson learned from a plate full of cheer,
Spaghetti together, nothing to fear.

Bliss Between the Strands

Between every strand, happiness twines,
In pasta's embrace, our laughter aligns.
Spaghetti as comfort, a warm sunny hug,
In this bowl of delight, we all feel snug.

With every good sauce, we mix and we play,
Crafting moments of joy in a glorious display.
A sprinkle of laughter, a dash of delight,
In this noodle pursuit, everything feels right.

So twirl up your hopes, let your fork be your pen,
In this silly culinary world, we're all friends.
Between every bite, let the fun intertwine,
In the bliss of the pasta, our spirits will shine.

So dinner is served, let the stories unfold,
With strands of connection, watch memories mold.
In every good meal, joy's recipe blends,
Between the noodles, the laughter never ends.

www.ingramcontent.com/pod-product-compliance
Lightning Source LLC
Chambersburg PA
CBHW051640160426
43209CB00004B/735